*Congressional
Research
Service*

The Consumer Financial Protection Bureau (CFPB): A Legal Analysis

David H. Carpenter
Legislative Attorney

June 7, 2012

Congressional Research Service
7-5700
www.crs.gov
R42572

Summary

In the wake of the worst U.S. financial crisis since the Great Depression, Congress passed and the President signed into law sweeping reforms of the financial services regulatory system through the Dodd-Frank Wall Street Reform and Consumer Protection Act (Dodd-Frank Act), P.L. 111-203.

Title X of the Dodd-Frank Act is entitled the Consumer Financial Protection Act of 2010 (CFP Act). The CFP Act establishes the Bureau of Consumer Financial Protection (CFPB or Bureau) within the Federal Reserve System (FRS) with rulemaking, enforcement, and supervisory powers over many consumer financial products and services, as well as the entities that sell them. The CFP Act significantly enhances federal consumer protection regulatory authority over nondepository financial institutions, potentially subjecting them to analogous supervisory, examination, and enforcement standards that have been applicable to depository institutions in the past. The act also transfers to the Bureau much of the consumer compliance authority over larger depositories that previously had been held by banking regulators. Additionally, the Bureau acquired the authority to write rules to implement most federal consumer financial protection laws that previously was held by a number of other federal agencies.

Although the powers that the CFPB has at its disposal are largely the same or analogous to those that other federal regulators have held for decades, there is a great deal of uncertainty in how the new agency will exercise these broad and flexible authorities, especially in light of its almost exclusive focus on consumer protection. As a result, the CFP Act has proven to be one of the more controversial portions of the financial reform legislation.

The 112th Congress is actively involved in conducting oversight of the implementation of the CFP Act. Additionally, the 112th Congress has considered a number of bills that would significantly alter the structure of the Bureau. For example, H.R. 2434, the Financial Services and General Government Appropriations Act, 2012, would make the CFPB's primary funding subject to the traditional appropriations process, and H.R. 1315, the Consumer Financial Protection Safety and Soundness Improvement Act, would convert the CFPB's leadership structure from a sole directorship to a commission and would allow the newly established Financial Stability Oversight Council (FSOC) to overturn CFPB-issued regulations with a simple majority vote, as opposed to the current super majority requirement. H.R. 2434 was reported favorably out of the House Committee on Appropriations, and H.R. 1315 was referred to the Senate Committee on Banking, Housing, and Urban Affairs after passing the full House by a vote of 241 to 173. Additionally, 44 Senators signed a letter to the President expressing support for the Bureau-related objectives of H.R. 2434 and H.R. 1315.

This report provides an overview of the regulatory structure of consumer finance under existing federal law before the Dodd-Frank Act went into effect and examines arguments for modifying the regime in order to more effectively regulate consumer financial markets. It then analyzes how the CFP Act changes that legal structure, with a focus on the Bureau's organization; the entities and activities that fall (and do not fall) under the Bureau's supervisory, enforcement, and rulemaking authorities; the Bureau's general and specific rulemaking powers and procedures; and the Bureau's funding.

Contents

Contacts

Introduction

In the wake of the worst U.S. financial crisis since the Great Depression, Congress passed and the President signed into law sweeping reforms of the financial services regulatory system through the Dodd-Frank Wall Street Reform and Consumer Protection Act (Dodd-Frank Act), P.L. 111-203.

Title X of the Dodd-Frank Act is entitled the Consumer Financial Protection Act of 2010 (CFP Act). The CFP Act establishes the Bureau of Consumer Financial Protection (CFPB or Bureau) within the Federal Reserve System (FRS) with rulemaking, enforcement, and supervisory powers over many consumer financial products and services, as well as the entities that sell them. The law also transfers to the Bureau the primary rulemaking authority over many federal consumer protection laws that, with one exception,[1] were enacted prior to the Dodd-Frank Act. These "enumerated consumer laws"[2] include the Truth in Lending Act[3] and the Real Estate Settlement Procedures Act.[4]

The CFP Act has proven to be one of the more controversial portions of the financial reform legislation. The 112th Congress is actively involved in conducting oversight of the implementation of the CFP Act.[5] Additionally, the 112th Congress has considered a number of bills that would significantly alter the structure of the Bureau. For example, H.R. 2434, the Financial Services and General Government Appropriations Act, 2012, would make the CFPB's primary funding subject to the traditional appropriations process, and H.R. 1315, the Consumer Financial Protection Safety and Soundness Improvement Act, would convert the CFPB's leadership structure from a sole directorship to a commission and would allow the newly established Financial Stability Oversight Council (FSOC) to overturn CFPB-issued regulations with a simple majority vote, as opposed to the current super majority requirement. H.R. 2434 was reported favorably out of the House Committee on Appropriations, and H.R. 1315 was referred to the Senate Committee on Banking, Housing, and Urban Affairs after passing the full House by a vote of 241 to 173. Additionally, 44 Senators signed a letter to the President expressing support for the Bureau-related objectives of H.R. 2434 and H.R. 1315.[6]

This report provides an overview of the regulatory structure of consumer finance under existing federal law before the Dodd-Frank Act went into effect and examines arguments for modifying the regime in order to more effectively regulate consumer financial markets. It then analyzes how the CFP Act changes that legal structure, with a focus on the Bureau's organization; the entities and activities that fall (and do not fall) under the Bureau's supervisory, enforcement, and rulemaking authorities; the Bureau's general and specific rulemaking powers and procedures; and the Bureau's funding.

---

[1] The Bureau acquired rulemaking authority pursuant to most provisions of the Mortgage Reform and Anti-Predatory Lending Act, which was enacted as Title XIV of the Dodd-Frank Act. Dodd-Frank Act §1400.

[2] Dodd-Frank Act §1002(12), 12 U.S.C. §5481(12).

[3] 15 U.S.C. §§1601, *et seq.*

[4] 12 U.S.C. §§2601, *et seq.*

[5] See, e.g., *Who's Watching the Watchmen? Oversight of the Consumer Financial Protection Bureau, Hearing Before the Subcomm. on TARP, Financial Services and Bailouts of Public and Private Programs of the Comm. on Oversight and Government Reform,* 112th Cong. (2011).

[6] *44 U.S. Sen. to Obama No Accountability, No Confirmation,* Sen. Richard Shelby, News Release, May 5, 2011, available at http://shelby.senate.gov/public/index.cfm/2011/5/44-u-s-sens-to-obama-no-accountability-no-confirmation.

Federal Consumer Financial Protection Regulation Before the CFPB

Before the CFP Act went into effect, which largely occurred on July 21, 2011 (called the "designated transfer date"),[7] the authority to write rules to implement the majority of the federal consumer financial protection laws, the power to enforce these laws, and the supervisory authority over the individuals and companies offering and selling consumer financial products and services were predominately shared by five different banking regulators, as well as the Federal Trade Commission (FTC) and the Department of Housing and Urban Development (HUD). The jurisdiction of these regulators varied based on the type of institution involved and, in some cases, based on the type of financial activities in which institutions engaged.

The authority of the five banking regulators varied based on depository charters. The Office of the Comptroller of the Currency (OCC) supervised national banks; the Board of Governors of the Federal Reserve System (FRB) supervised domestic operations of foreign banks and state-chartered banks that were members of the FRS; the Federal Deposit Insurance Corporation (FDIC) supervised state-chartered banks and other state-chartered banking institutions that were not members of the FRS;[8] the National Credit Union Administration (NCUA) supervised federally insured credit unions; and the Office of Thrift Supervision (OTS)[9] supervised federal savings and loan associations and thrifts. The five banking regulators were charged with the two-pronged mandate of regulating for both safety and soundness, as well as consumer compliance. Safety and soundness regulation, also referred to as prudential regulation, consists of ensuring that institutions are managed in a safe and sound manner so as to maintain profitability and avoid failure.[10] The focus of consumer compliance regulation, on the other hand, is ensuring that institutions are in compliance with applicable consumer protection and fair lending laws.[11]

To reach these ends, the banking regulators were provided with broad authority to subject banks, credit unions, and thrifts (which this report will collectively refer to as "depository institutions" or "depositories") to up-front regulatory standards, such as maintaining minimum capital levels, through regulations, orders, and guidelines. These regulators also were given strong supervisory powers, including the authority to perform on-site examinations of depositories,[12] and flexible enforcement powers to rectify problems found during the course of their supervision.[13] These supervisory powers gave banking regulators at least the potential to catch problems before they caused significant harm to consumers, counterparties, and the depositories themselves.

---

[7] Designated Transfer Date, 75 Fed. Reg. 57,252 (Sept. 20, 2010).

[8] The FDIC, which administers the Deposit Insurance Fund, also has certain regulatory powers over state and national banks holding FDIC-insured deposits; however, these authorities generally are secondary to the institution's primary federal regulator. See, e.g., 12 U.S.C. §1820.

[9] The Dodd-Frank Act eliminated the OTS and transferred its powers to the OCC, FDIC, FRB, and CFPB.

[10] Heidi Mandanis Schooner, *Consuming Debt Structuring the Federal Response to Abuses in Consumer Credit*, 18 Loy. Consumer L. Rev. 43, 52-53 (2005).

[11] *Id.* at 50, 54-55.

[12] All depositories generally must be examined at least once every 18 months, but the largest depositories have examiners on-site on a continuous basis. See, e.g., 12 U.S.C. §1820(d).

[13] 12 U.S.C. §§1818 and 1831o.

Additionally, consumer compliance issues often were dealt with informally and confidentially as part of the examination process, rather than through public, *ex post* formal enforcement orders.[14]

The Federal Trade Commission (FTC) was the primary federal regulator for nondepository financial institutions, such as payday lenders and mortgage brokers.[15] Unlike the federal banking regulators, the FTC had little up-front supervisory or enforcement authority. The FTC's powers generally were limited to *ex post* enforcement. Thus, the FTC did not have the statutory authority to regularly examine nondepository financial institutions or impose reporting requirements on them as a way to proactively ensure they were complying with consumer protection laws. The FTC also did not have any direct safety and soundness authority over institutions.[16] Instead, nondepository financial institutions were primarily supervised by state regulators. The powers granted to state regulators and the level of supervision these regulators provided varied considerably from state to state.

In addition to institution-based distinctions, both depository and nondepository financial institutions also were subject to the restrictions of federal consumer financial protection laws. These federal laws each regulate specific types of consumer products and activities. For example, the Truth in Lending Act (TILA)[17] requires disclosures regarding the terms and conditions associated with extensions of consumer credit; the Equal Credit Opportunity Act (ECOA)[18] bans certain kinds of discrimination in consumer lending; the Real Estate Settlement Procedures Act of 1974 (RESPA)[19] imposes disclosure requirements and fee restrictions associated with home loan settlements; the Truth in Savings Act (TISA)[20] requires disclosures regarding the terms and conditions of consumer deposit accounts; and the Fair Debt Collection Practices Act (FDCPA)[21] restricts third-party debt collection activities.[22]

---

[14] See, e.g., Office of the Comptroller of the Currency, Comptroller's Handbook for Bank Supervision Process, pp. 46-47 (2007), available at http://www.occ.gov/publications/publications-by-type/comptrollers-handbook/_pdf/banksupervisionprocess.pdf; Board of Governors of the Federal Reserve System, Commercial Bank Examination Manual §5040.1 (2011), available at http://federalreserve.gov/boarddocs/supmanual/supervision_cbem.htm. See, also, In re Subpoena Served upon Comptroller of Currency, 967 F.2d 630, 633-634 (D.C. Cir. 1992) (discussing the bank examination privilege: "Bank safety and soundness supervision is an iterative process of comment by the regulators and response by the bank. The success of the supervision therefore depends vitally upon the quality of communication between the regulated banking firm and the bank regulatory agency. This relationship is both extensive and informal. It is extensive in that bank examiners concern themselves with all manner of a bank's affairs: Not only the classification of assets and the review of financial transactions, but also the adequacy of security systems and of internal reporting requirements, and even the quality of managerial personnel are of concern to the examiners. The supervisory relationship is informal in the sense that it calls for adjustment, not adjudication. In the process of comment and response, the bank may agree to change some aspect of its operation or accounting; alternatively, if the bank and the examiners reach impasse, then their dispute may be elevated for resolution at higher levels within the bank regulatory agency. It is the very rare dispute, however, that culminates in any formal action, such as a cease and desist order." (internal citations omitted)).

[15] The FTC also serves as the primary federal regulator for many non-financial commercial enterprises.

[16] Heidi Mandanis Schooner, *Consuming Debt Structuring the Federal Response to Abuses in Consumer Credit*, 18 Loy. Consumer L. Rev. 43, 56-58 (2005). See also Fed. Trade Comm'n Operating Manual, Ch. 1, available at http://www.ftc.gov/foia/ch01overview.pdf.

[17] 15 U.S.C. §§1601, *et seq.*

[18] 15 U.S.C. §§1691, *et seq.*

[19] 12 U.S.C. §§2601, *et seq.*

[20] 12 U.S.C. §§4301, *et seq.*

[21] 15 U.S.C. §§1692, *et seq.*

[22] Other federal consumer protection laws include the Consumer Leasing Act of 1976 (15 U.S.C. §§1667 *et seq.*), (continued...)

Individually, these enumerated consumer laws target discrete activities. Taken as a whole, they govern a broad and diverse set of consumer activities and services.[23] Before the Dodd-Frank Act went into effect, the rulemaking authority to implement federal consumer financial protection laws was largely held by the FRB.[24] The authority to enforce the federal consumer financial protection laws and regulations, however, was spread among all of the banking regulators, the FTC, and HUD.[25]

In short, the banking regulators held both prudential and consumer compliance supervisory and enforcement powers over depository institutions. Although they had the authority to take *ex post* enforcement actions, the banking regulators placed a great deal of emphasis on *ex ante* regulation and supervision. The FTC was the primary regulator of nondepository financial institutions. The FTC's authority was much more limited than that of the banking regulators. Its authority was almost exclusively limited to *ex post* enforcement.[26] Additionally, both depositories and nondepository financial institutions were required to comply with the various federal consumer financial laws and the regulations issued under those laws. The rulemaking authority under the federal consumer financial laws was predominately held by the FRB, but the authority to enforce those laws and regulations was spread among all the banking regulators, as well as the FTC and HUD.[27]

Arguments for Consolidating Federal Consumer Financial Regulatory Powers

Scholars and consumer advocates argued that the complex, fragmented federal consumer financial protection regulatory system in place before the Dodd-Frank Act failed to adequately protect consumers and created market inefficiencies to the detriment of both financial institutions and consumers. Some argued that these problems could be corrected if all federal consumer financial regulatory powers were consolidated in a single regulator with a consumer focus.[28] As

---

(...continued)

which requires certain disclosures for consumer leases; the Electronic Funds Transfer Act (15 U.S.C. §§1693 *et seq.*), which establishes consumer protections regarding electronic fund transfers; the Fair Credit Billing Act (15 U.S.C. §§1666, *et seq.*), which establishes consumer protections regarding billing errors associated with extensions of credit; and the Fair Credit Reporting Act (15 U.S.C. §§1681, *et seq.*), which governs consumer credit histories and data collection.

[23] Oren Bar-Gill and Elizabeth Warren, *Making Credit Safer*, 157 U. of Penn. L. Rev. 1, 83-85 (Nov. 2008). The activities and services that are covered by the enumerated consumer laws include debt collection practices; debit card transfers; overdraft services; consumer leases; mortgage lending; credit card lending; mortgage appraisals; real estate settlement practices; and credit reporting.

[24] To a lesser extent, other agencies held rulemaking authority under federal consumer laws. For example, rulemaking authority under RESPA was held by HUD.

[25] Heidi Mandanis Schooner, *Consuming Debt Structuring the Federal Response to Abuses in Consumer Credit*, 18 Loy. Consumer L. Rev. 43, 56-58 (2005); Oren Bar-Gill and Elizabeth Warren, *Making Credit Safer*, 157 U. of Penn. L. Rev. 1, 86-97 (Nov. 2008).

[26] *Id.* See also Fed. Trade Comm'n Operating Manual, Ch. 1, available at http://www.ftc.gov/foia/ch01overview.pdf.

[27] Oren Bar-Gill and Elizabeth Warren, *Making Credit Safer*, 157 U. of Penn. L. Rev. 1, 94-97 (Nov. 2008).

[28] See, e.g., Heidi Mandanis Schooner, *Consuming Debt Structuring the Federal Response to Abuses in Consumer Credit*, 18 Loy. Consumer L. Rev. 43, 82 (2005) ("The most sensible approach to correcting the structural defect in the current regime would be to eliminate entirely the federal banking regulators' role in consumer protection. This approach has the potential to enhance both the fairness and the efficiency of the current system. This proposal would create a more fair system because banks and non-banks would be treated alike. This would level the playing field (continued...)

---

discussed below, proponents of change generally raised two primary criticisms of the pre-Dodd-Frank Act regulatory system. One was that it allowed financial institutions to engage in "regulatory arbitrage," which pressured regulators to lower supervisory standards in a so-called "race-to-the-bottom."[29] The other was that banking regulators tended to place greater emphasis on their safety and soundness duties than their consumer compliance responsibilities.[30]

"Regulatory Arbitrage" Resulted in a "Race-to-the-Bottom"

"Regulatory arbitrage," that is, a financial institution's ability to take advantage of regulatory loopholes or permissive supervisory oversight, arguably resulted from three forms of competition—competition between depositories and nondepositories; competition between the various types of depository charters (e.g., state charter versus federal charter; bank charter versus thrift charter); and competition between the financial regulators.[31] These competitive pressures were fueled by the fact that there is considerable overlap in the types of consumer products and services that are offered by state and federal depositories, as well as by nondepository institutions. However, as described in detail above, these institutions had different federal regulators and could be subject to very different regulatory regimes.[32]

Some believed that the more costly supervisory burdens of depositories gave nondepositories a competitive advantage over depository institutions in certain consumer markets.[33] The general

---

(...continued)

among providers of similar financial services. In addition, this proposal provides many potential efficiencies that derive from the recognition of consumer protection as a distinct regulatory goal from prudential regulation."); Oren Bar-Gill and Elizabeth Warren, *Making Credit Safer*, 157 U. of Penn. L. Rev. 1, 98-100 (Nov. 2008).

[29] *Regulatory Restructuring- Safeguarding Consumer Protection and the Role of the Federal Reserve Hearing Before the Subcomm. on Domestic Monetary Policy & Tech. of the H. Comm. on Fin. Servs.*, 111th Cong. (2009) (written testimony of Patricia A. McCoy, Director of the Insurance Law Center and George J. and Helen M. England Professor of Law at the University of Connecticut School of Law), available at http://archives.financialservices.house.gov/media/file/hearings/111/mccoy_house_testimony—hearing—july_16_2009.pdf; Adam J. Levitan, *The Consumer Financial Protection Agency*, The PEW Financial Reform Project Briefing Paper # 3, pp. 6-7 (2009), available at http://www.pewtrusts.org/uploadedFiles/wwwpewtrustsorg/Reports/Financial_Reform/Pew-Levitan-CFPA.pdf; Oren Bar-Gill and Elizabeth Warren, *Making Credit Safer*, 157 U. of Penn. L. Rev. 1, 82-84 (Nov. 2008).

[30] Adam J. Levitan, *The Consumer Financial Protection Agency*, The PEW Financial Reform Project Briefing Paper # 3, p. 4 (2009), available at http://www.pewtrusts.org/uploadedFiles/wwwpewtrustsorg/Reports/Financial_Reform/Pew-Levitan-CFPA.pdf; Oren Bar-Gill and Elizabeth Warren, *Making Credit Safer*, 157 U. of Penn. L. Rev. 1, 90 (Nov. 2008); Heidi Mandanis Schooner, *The Role of Central Banks in Bank Supervision in the United States and the United Kingdom*, 28 Brook. J. of Int'l L 411, 427 (2003) ("the Federal Reserve's ... regulatory role remains focused on safety and soundness and not on other goals of financial regulation, such as consumer protection.").

[31] *Regulatory Restructuring- Safeguarding Consumer Protection and the Role of the Federal Reserve Hearing Before the Subcomm. on Domestic Monetary Policy & Tech. of the H. Comm. on Fin. Servs.*, 111th Cong. (2009) (written testimony of Patricia A. McCoy, Director of the Insurance Law Center and George J. and Helen M. England Professor of Law at the University of Connecticut School of Law), available at http://archives.financialservices.house.gov/media/file/hearings/111/mccoy_house_testimony—hearing—july_16_2009.pdf; Adam J. Levitan, *The Consumer Financial Protection Agency*, The PEW Financial Reform Project Briefing Paper # 3, pp. 6-7 (2009), available at http://www.pewtrusts.org/uploadedFiles/wwwpewtrustsorg/Reports/Financial_Reform/Pew-Levitan-CFPA.pdf; Oren Bar-Gill and Elizabeth Warren, *Making Credit Safer*, 157 U. of Penn. L. Rev. 1, 82-84 (Nov. 2008).

[32] *Id.*

[33] *Regulatory Restructuring- Safeguarding Consumer Protection and the Role of the Federal Reserve Hearing Before the Subcomm. on Domestic Monetary Policy & Tech. of the H. Comm. on Fin. Servs.*, 111th Cong. (2009) (written testimony of Patricia A. McCoy, Director of the Insurance Law Center and George J. and Helen M. England Professor of Law at the University of Connecticut School of Law), available at http://archives.financialservices.house.gov/media/file/hearings/111/mccoy_house_testimony—hearing—july_16_2009.pdf; Heidi Mandanis Schooner, *Consuming Debt* (continued...)

---

discrepancy may have encouraged banking regulators to lower their supervisory standards as a way to help depositories under their jurisdictions more effectively compete with nondepositories.[34]

Banking regulators may have been further pressured to relax regulatory scrutiny because of the threat that depositories would change their charters. Although there were significant distinctions between the various depository charters historically, statutory changes over the years have eliminated many of those differences.[35] As a result, many depositories could change their charters without having to significantly alter their business practices.[36] One of the few remaining differences was that the depository charters determined an institution's primary regulator. Thus, an influencing factor in an institution's chartering decision could be the characteristics of the regulator associated with a particular charter. Financial institutions may be incentivized to switch their charters in order to be supervised by the agency with the lightest, least costly regulatory touch.[37]

(...continued)

Structuring the Federal Response to Abuses in Consumer Credit, 18 Loy. Consumer L. Rev. 43, 82 (2005).

[34] See, e.g., *Regulatory Restructuring- Safeguarding Consumer Protection and the Role of the Federal Reserve Hearing Before the Subcomm. on Domestic Monetary Policy & Tech. of the H. Comm. on Fin. Servs.*, 111th Cong. (2009) (written testimony of Patricia A. McCoy, Director of the Insurance Law Center and George J. and Helen M. England Professor of Law at the University of Connecticut School of Law), available at http://archives.financialservices.house.gov/media/file/hearings/111/mccoy_house_testimony—hearing—july_16_2009.pdf ("This dual regulatory system allowed mortgage lender [*sic.*] to play regulators off one another by threatening to change charters. Mortgage lenders are free to operate with or without depository institution charters. Similarly, depository institutions can choose between a state and federal charter and between a thrift charter and a commercial bank charter. Each of these choices allows a lender to change regulators. A lender could escape a strict state law by switching to a federal bank or thrift charter or by shifting its operations to a less regulated state. Similarly, a lender could escape a strict regulator by converting its charter to one with a more accommodating regulator."). See, also, Heidi Mandanis Schooner, *Consuming Debt Structuring the Federal Response to Abuses in Consumer Credit*, 18 Loy. Consumer L. Rev. 43, 82 (2005). It should be noted, however, that depositories receive benefits that generally are not available to nondepositories, and these benefits may offset the distinctions in regulatory burdens, to some degree. These benefits include federal deposit insurance and access to the Federal Reserve's discount window lending facility. 12 U.S.C. §§1815 (deposit insurance), 343 (discount window).

[35] Dain C. Donelson and David Zaring, *Charter Switching and the Financial Crisis Evidence from the Office of Thrift Supervision*, pp. 11-18 (Oct. 13, 2009) (unpublished paper for the Illinois Corporate Law Symposium), available at http://www.law.illinois.edu/_shared/pdfs/thrift%20chartering%20draft%2010%20dz.docx.

[36] *Id.* at 8 ("From 1998-2008, OTS lost a net 45 institutions as more thrifts converted to banks than did banks to thrifts. Moreover, some financial institutions have left the federal system altogether. Between 2000 and 2008, at least 30 financial institutions gave up their federal charters and obtained state charters." (internal citations omitted)). See, also, Oren Bar-Gill and Elizabeth Warren, *Making Credit Safer*, 157 U. of Penn. L. Rev. 1, 82-84 (Nov. 2008).

[37] *The Financial Crisis Inquiry Report*, Fin. Crisis Inquiry Comm'n, p. *xviii*, Jan. 2011, available at http://www.gpo.gov/fdsys/pkg/GPO-FCIC/pdf/GPO-FCIC.pdf; Dain C. Donelson and David Zaring, *Charter Switching and the Financial Crisis Evidence from the Office of Thrift Supervision*, pp. 4-5 (Oct. 13, 2009) (unpublished paper for the Illinois Corporate Law Symposium), available at http://www.law.illinois.edu/_shared/pdfs/thrift%20chartering%20draft%2010%20dz.docx ("We also observe that those institutions that switched their charter to OTS during the period of our study had, because of the way the differences between the bank charter and the thrift charter dissipated over time, probably only did so because they preferred being regulated by OTS, rather than because they preferred the business model legislatively required of thrifts (non-thrifts could pursue that model without any legal deficiency or cost)."); *Regulatory Restructuring- Safeguarding Consumer Protection and the Role of the Federal Reserve Hearing Before the Subcomm. on Domestic Monetary Policy & Tech. of the H. Comm. on Fin. Servs.*, 111th Cong. (2009) (written testimony of Patricia A. McCoy, Director of the Insurance Law Center and George J. and Helen M. England Professor of Law at the University of Connecticut School of Law), available at http://archives.financialservices.house.gov/media/file/hearings/111/mccoy_house_testimony—hearing—july_16_2009.pdf; Adam J. Levitan, *The Consumer Financial Protection Agency*, The PEW Financial Reform Project Briefing Paper # 3, pp. 6-7 (2009), available at http://www.pewtrusts.org/uploadedFiles/wwwpewtrustsorg/Reports/ (continued...)

Banking regulators also had a financial incentive to attract institutions to their charters and to ensure the happiness of institutions already within their supervisory jurisdictions because a significant portion of their budgets derive from assessments against the institutions under their supervision.[38] As a result, if one banking regulator lowered its regulatory standards as a way to encourage financial institutions to change their charters, the others may have been pressured to respond in kind.[39]

Some argued that these competitive forces placed downward pressure on regulators, which led to a "race-to-the-bottom."[40] Therefore, some proposed consolidating consumer compliance regulatory authority in a single agency as a means to level the regulatory playing field for depositories and nondepository financial institutions, thus preventing the "race-to-the-bottom" and "regulatory arbitrage" to the benefit of both consumers and financial institutions.[41]

(...continued)

Financial_Reform/Pew-Levitan-CFPA.pdf; Oren Bar-Gill and Elizabeth Warren, *Making Credit Safer*, 157 U. of Penn. L. Rev. 1, 93-94 (Nov. 2008).

[38] See, e.g., Oren Bar-Gill and Elizabeth Warren, *Making Credit Safer*, 157 U. of Penn. L. Rev. 1, 93-94 (Nov. 2008) ("The OCC's inaction may also be attributable, at least in part, to its direct financial stake in keeping its bank clients happy. Large national banks fund a significant portion of the OCC's budget. ... By attracting more financial-services companies to incorporate as federally chartered banks under the supervision of the OCC, the agency can expand its influence. Accordingly, the OCC would be reluctant to impose substantial constraints on banks, fearing that such constraints might induce the banks to switch to a competing regulator." (internal citations omitted)). See, also, Adam J. Levitan, *The Consumer Financial Protection Agency*, The PEW Financial Reform Project Briefing Paper # 3, pp. 6-7 (2009), available at http://www.pewtrusts.org/uploadedFiles/wwwpewtrustsorg/Reports/Financial_Reform/Pew-Levitan-CFPA.pdf.

[39] At least one scholar believes that "regulatory arbitrage" was the primary reason why Countrywide, N.A., the bank subsidiary of what was once the largest mortgage lender in the country, converted from an OCC-regulated national bank to an OTS-regulated thrift in 2007.See, e.g., *Regulatory Restructuring- Safeguarding Consumer Protection and the Role of the Federal Reserve Hearing Before the Subcomm. on Domestic Monetary Policy & Tech. of the H. Comm. on Fin. Servs.*, 111th Cong. (2009) (written testimony of Patricia A. McCoy, Director of the Insurance Law Center and George J. and Helen M. England Professor of Law at the University of Connecticut School of Law), available at http://archives.financialservices.house.gov/media/file/hearings/111/mccoy_house_testimony—hearing—july_16_2009.pdf. After the charter conversion, Countrywide, N.A. became Countrywide, F.S.B. Countrywide Financial Corporation, the parent company of Countrywide, F.S.B., has since been acquired by Bank of America, Corporation. See, the historical bank profile of Countrywide, N.A., available at http://www2.fdic.gov/IDASP/main_bankfind.asp.

[40] *Regulatory Restructuring- Safeguarding Consumer Protection and the Role of the Federal Reserve Hearing Before the Subcomm. on Domestic Monetary Policy & Tech. of the H. Comm. on Fin. Servs.*, 111th Cong. (2009) (written testimony of Patricia A. McCoy, Director of the Insurance Law Center and George J. and Helen M. England Professor of Law at the University of Connecticut School of Law), available at http://archives.financialservices.house.gov/media/file/hearings/111/mccoy_house_testimony—hearing—july_16_2009.pdf; Adam J. Levitan, *The Consumer Financial Protection Agency*, The PEW Financial Reform Project Briefing Paper # 3, pp. 6-7 (2009), available at http://www.pewtrusts.org/uploadedFiles/wwwpewtrustsorg/Reports/Financial_Reform/Pew-Levitan-CFPA.pdf; Oren Bar-Gill and Elizabeth Warren, *Making Credit Safer*, 157 U. of Penn. L. Rev. 1, 98 (Nov. 2008).

[41] *Regulatory Restructuring- Safeguarding Consumer Protection and the Role of the Federal Reserve Hearing Before the Subcomm. on Domestic Monetary Policy & Tech. of the H. Comm. on Fin. Servs.*, 111th Cong. (2009) (written testimony of Patricia A. McCoy, Director of the Insurance Law Center and George J. and Helen M. England Professor of Law at the University of Connecticut School of Law), available at http://archives.financialservices.house.gov/media/file/hearings/111/mccoy_house_testimony—hearing—july_16_2009.pdf; Adam J. Levitan, *The Consumer Financial Protection Agency*, The PEW Financial Reform Project Briefing Paper # 3, pp. 7-8 (2009), available at http://www.pewtrusts.org/uploadedFiles/wwwpewtrustsorg/Reports/Financial_Reform/Pew-Levitan-CFPA.pdf; Oren Bar-Gill and Elizabeth Warren, *Making Credit Safer*, 157 U. of Penn. L. Rev. 1, 98-100 (Nov. 2008).

Safety and Soundness Historically Have Trumped Consumer Compliance

The second major criticism of the federal consumer financial protection regulatory system before the Dodd-Frank Act was that no federal agency had both the mission and legal authority to effectively regulate consumer markets.[42] The banking regulators had the statutory powers to protect consumers; however, it has been argued that the banking regulators placed more importance on their safety and soundness mission than on their consumer protection duties. Scholars have noted that the banking regulators view their primary mission as protecting the safety and soundness of banks, not protecting consumers.[43] This heightened focus on safety and soundness arguably caused regulators to turn a blind eye toward practices that may have been detrimental to consumers if those practices were profitable for banks. This safety and soundness-centric mission also may have hampered the banking regulators' ability to hire and retain staff with expertise in consumer products and consumer behavior.[44]

The FTC, on the other hand, did have a consumer focus. However, the FTC's statutory authority prevented it from conducting *ex ante* supervision of nondepositories and from regulating depositories altogether.[45] Some argued that these statutory limitations precluded the FTC from sufficiently protecting consumers and eliminating consumer financial market inefficiencies.[46]

Professors Warren and Bar-Gill summed up these arguments this way:

> Effective regulation requires both authority and motivation. Yet none of the many regulators in the consumer credit field satisfies these basic requirements. Federal banking regulators have the authority but not the motivation. For each federal banking agency, consumer protection is not first (or even second) on its priority list. By contrast, the FTC makes consumer protection a priority, but it enjoys only limited authority over consumer credit markets.[47]

Thus, it was argued that consumer markets could be effectively regulated if a federal agency was established with both a consumer protection focus and strong supervisory, enforcement, and rulemaking powers.

---

[42] Adam J. Levitan, *The Consumer Financial Protection Agency*, The PEW Financial Reform Project Briefing Paper # 3, p. 4 (2009), available at http://www.pewtrusts.org/uploadedFiles/wwwpewtrustsorg/Reports/Financial_Reform/Pew-Levitan-CFPA.pdf; Oren Bar-Gill and Elizabeth Warren, *Making Credit Safer*, 157 U. of Penn. L. Rev. 1, 90 (Nov. 2008); Heidi Mandanis Schooner, *The Role of Central Banks in Bank Supervision in the United States and the United Kingdom*, 28 Brook. J. of Int'l L 411, 427 (2003) ("the Federal Reserve's ... regulatory role remains focused on safety and soundness and not on other goals of financial regulation, such as consumer protection.").

[43] *Id.*

[44] Adam J. Levitan, *The Consumer Financial Protection Agency*, The PEW Financial Reform Project Briefing Paper # 3, p. 5 (2009), available at http://www.pewtrusts.org/uploadedFiles/wwwpewtrustsorg/Reports/Financial_Reform/Pew-Levitan-CFPA.pdf.

[45] Oren Bar-Gill and Elizabeth Warren, *Making Credit Safer*, 157 U. of Penn. L. Rev. 1, 95-97 (Nov. 2008); Heidi Mandanis Schooner, *Consuming Debt Structuring the Federal Response to Abuses in Consumer Credit*, 18 Loy. Consumer L. Rev. 43, 56-58 (2005).

[46] Oren Bar-Gill and Elizabeth Warren, *Making Credit Safer*, 157 U. of Penn. L. Rev. 1, 95-97 (Nov. 2008); Heidi Mandanis Schooner, *Consuming Debt Structuring the Federal Response to Abuses in Consumer Credit*, 18 Loy. Consumer L. Rev. 43, 82-83 (2005).

[47] Oren Bar-Gill and Elizabeth Warren, *Making Credit Safer*, 157 U. of Penn. L. Rev. 1, 85-86 (Nov. 2008).

Overview of the Bureau

The CFP Act significantly alters the consumer financial protection landscape by consolidating rulemaking authority and, to a lesser extent, supervisory and enforcement authority in one regulator—the CFPB. The CFP Act empowers the Bureau through the transfer of existing consumer protection powers from other federal regulators and the establishment of heightened consumer protection authorities not previously held by federal regulators. The Bureau has jurisdiction over an array of consumer financial products and services, and it serves as the primary federal consumer financial supervisor of many of the institutions that offer these products and services. However, at least six other agencies—the OCC, FRB, FDIC, NCUA, FTC, and HUD—will continue to hold some consumer protection powers.

The CFP Act also imposes certain limitations on the Bureau's authority to regulate various types of financial institutions and financial activities. Several fundamental policy questions arose consistently during the legislative debate over proposals that ultimately became the CFP Act. These policy questions seem to be the primary motivations for the exceptions to the consolidation of consumer protection power in the CFPB and the various restrictions on the Bureau's authorities.

One policy question was how best to balance the safety and soundness regulation of depositories with that of consumer compliance. There is considerable overlap between prudential and consumer compliance regulation.[48] For instance, a mortgage that the borrower is unable to fully repay is typically bad for both the borrower and the lender. The borrower runs the risk of damage to her credit score and the loss of her home. The lender may suffer from lost interest income and increased costs associated with the foreclosure process. However, there are some areas in which there can be a conflict between safety and soundness regulation and consumer protection. When a banking activity is profitable, safety and soundness regulators tend to look upon it favorably because it enables the bank to meet capital requirements and withstand financial shocks. A consumer protection regulator, on the other hand, may look at such activity less favorably if the profit is seen to have been gained unfairly or deceptively at the expense of consumers.[49]

A related question that surfaced frequently during the legislative debate is the extent to which large and small financial institutions should be treated differently in the regulatory structure.[50] Whereas the largest depository institutions are accustomed to having examiners on-site continuously, examinations may be more disruptive for smaller depositories.[51] Enhanced

---

[48] Heidi Mandanis Schooner, *Consuming Debt Structuring the Federal Response to Abuses in Consumer Credit*, 18 Loy. Consumer L. Rev. 43, 62-63 (2005).

[49] *Id.* at 67-69; Oren Bar-Gill and Elizabeth Warren, *Making Credit Safer*, 157 U. of Penn. L. Rev. 1, 90-94 (Nov. 2008).

[50] See, e.g., October 2, 2009, Discussion Draft of the Over-the-Counter Derivatives Markets Act of 2009; September 25, 2009, Discussion Draft of the Consumer Financial Protection Agency Act of 2009 (to be reported as H.R. 3126); H.R. 3763, to amend the Fair Credit Reporting Act to provide for an exclusion from Red Flag Guidelines for certain businesses; and H.R. 3639, Expedited CARD Reform for Consumers Act of 2009, Markup of the H. Comm. on Fin. Services, 111th Cong. (2009), webcasts available at http://archives.financialservices.house.gov/Hearings/ hearingDetails.aspx?NewsID=801.

[51] Sarah Bloom Raskin, Gov., Bd. of Gov. of the Fed. Reserve Sys., *Community Bank Examination and Supervision amid Economic Recovery*, speech at the Maryland Bankers Association First Friday Economic Outlook Forum, Jan. 6, 2012, available at http://www.federalreserve.gov/newsevents/speech/raskin20120106a.pdf; *FDIC Oversight Examining and Evaluating the Role of the Regulator During the Financial Crisis and Today, Hearing Before the* (continued...)

---

compliance costs also are likely to more significantly impact smaller depositories, with their lower aggregate revenues, than larger depositories. Similar arguments could be made for large versus small nondepository financial institutions. Additionally, when assessing the causes of the recent financial crisis, many tend to place more blame on this country's large financial institutions than on smaller ones.[52] Thus, one could argue that the larger institutions should be subject to greater, more costly regulation than smaller institutions. On the other hand, the goal of the Dodd-Frank Act appears to be geared not just toward eliminating the exact causes of the recent financial crisis, but also toward preventing future crises.

Another issue that the legislative drafters of the CFP Act had to grapple with is that there is not always a clear delineation between financial and nonfinancial goods, services, and providers in the marketplace. For example, a clothing store's main line of business likely is selling clothes and shoes, so it may seem that a consumer financial regulator would have no regulatory role over it. However, most clothing retailers do rely on financial services to maintain their businesses. They usually accept credit cards and debit cards as a form of payment. Many clothing stores team with financial institutions to offer credit cards that provide store rewards for using the card. Clothing retailers also commonly offer electronic gift cards. Additionally, some clothing stores may directly offer financing options for the purchase of their merchandise. As a result, defining the scope of the Bureau's authority required careful consideration. In some instances, the act uses rigid, bright-line rules that provide considerable certainty as to where the Bureau's authorities begin and end. In other instances, the CFP Act imposes subjective standards intended to give the CFPB the flexibility to evolve with consumer financial markets, but that also create the potential that the Bureau will overreach by regulating beyond congressional intent.

Apparently as a result of the policy considerations outlined above, the act's allocation of regulatory authority among the prudential regulators and the CFPB varies based on institution size and type. Regulatory authority differs for (1) depository institutions with more than $10 billion in assets (i.e., "larger depositories"); (2) depository institutions with $10 billion or less in assets (i.e., "smaller depositories"); and (3) nondepositories. The Dodd-Frank Act also explicitly exempts a number of different entities and consumer financial activities from the CFPB's supervisory, enforcement, and rulemaking authorities.

Consequently, compliance costs and the extent to which the cost and availability of credit will be affected by the new regulator will depend on the type of institution that is providing consumer financial products and services, as well as exactly how the Bureau wields its powers and how aggressively it (and other state and federal regulators) enforces consumer protection laws and regulations.

(...continued)

Subcomm. on Fin. Inst. and Consumer Credit of the H. Comm. on Fin. Serv., 112th Cong. (2011) (written statement of Sheila C. Bair, Chairman, Fed. Deposit Ins. Corp.), available at http://financialservices.house.gov/UploadedFiles/052611bair.pdf.

[52] See, e.g., Ben S. Bernanke, Chairman, Bd. of Gov. of the Fed. Reserve Sys., *The Financial Crisis and Community Banking*, speech at the Independent Community Bankers of America's National Convention and Techworld, Mar. 20, 2009, available at http://www.federalreserve.gov/newsevents/speech/bernanke20090320a.htm ("Many of you likely are frustrated, and rightfully so, by the impact that the financial crisis and economic downturn has had on your banks, as well as on the reputation of bankers more generally. You may well have built your reputations and institutions through responsible lending and community-focused operations, but nonetheless, you now find yourselves facing higher deposit insurance assessments and increasing public skepticism about the behavior of bankers—outcomes that you perceive were largely caused by the actions of larger financial institutions.")

The breadth of the CFPB's supervisory, enforcement, and rulemaking powers is similar to that of the banking regulators. The banking regulators, however, have held those authorities for decades, which has established a certain level of certainty in the industry as to how those powers will be exercised. The fact that the CFPB does not have the same rich history coupled with the Bureau's overarching focus on consumers, as opposed to safety and soundness, has some anxious that the Bureau will overreach in utilizing its broad and flexible powers, which could lead to an excessive restriction in consumer credit and an undue increase in regulatory costs.[53]

Bureau's Purpose and Structure

The stated goal of the Bureau is to

> implement and, where applicable, enforce Federal consumer financial law consistently for the purpose of ensuring that all consumers have access to markets for consumer financial products and services and that markets for consumer financial products and services are fair, transparent, and competitive.[54]

The Bureau is established within the FRS, but it has a considerable amount of independence from the FRB. For instance, the FRB does not have the formal authority to stop, delay, or disapprove of a Bureau regulation, nor can it

> (A) intervene in any matter or proceeding before the Director [of the CFPB], including examinations or enforcement actions, unless otherwise specifically provided by law;
>
> (B) appoint, direct, or remove any officer or employee of the Bureau; or
>
> (C) merge or consolidate the Bureau, or any of the functions or responsibilities of the Bureau, with any division or office of the Board of Governors or the Federal reserve banks.[55]

The Bureau's authorities are concentrated within a single Director, rather than in a board or commission. The Director is to be appointed by the President, subject to the advice and consent of the Senate, to serve for a five-year term from which he could only be removed for "inefficiency, neglect of duty or malfeasance in office."[56] The Director has authority to hire the employees necessary to carry out the duties of the Bureau[57] and to delegate powers to employees.[58] This structure insulates the Bureau from the Office of the President and allows the Director to steer the course of the CFPB.[59] The Bureau's structure is similar to that of the OCC, which is established

[53] See, e.g., *44 U.S. Sen. to Obama No Accountability, No Confirmation*, Sen. Richard Shelby, News Release, May 5, 2011, available at http://shelby.senate.gov/public/index.cfm/2011/5/44-u-s-sens-to-obama-no-accountability-no-confirmation.

[54] Dodd-Frank Act §1021, 12 U.S.C. §5511.

[55] Dodd-Frank Act §1012, 12 U.S.C. §5492. The Chairman of the FRB, however, does serve as a voting member of the Financial Stability Oversight Council (FSOC) that has the authority to stay and overturn certain regulations issued by the Bureau. Dodd-Frank Act §111, 12 U.S.C. §5321(b). For a more detailed discussion of the FSOC's authority over CFPB regulations, see the "General Rulemaking Powers" section of this report.

[56] Dodd-Frank Act §1011, 12 U.S.C. §5491.

[57] Dodd-Frank Act §1013, 12 U.S.C. §5493.

[58] Dodd-Frank Act §1012, 12 U.S.C. §5492.

[59] On January 4, 2012, President Obama appointed Richard Cordray to be the first CFPB Director. Cordray's appointment raises a number of significant legal questions regarding the scope of the President's authority under the (continued...)

within the Department of the Treasury and is headed by a single individual, the Comptroller of the Currency.[60]

The law requires the Director to establish units within the Bureau to focus on consumer financial research; to provide guidance and technical assistance to traditionally underserved areas and individuals; and to monitor and to respond to consumer complaints. The act also requires the establishment of an Office of Fair Lending and Equal Opportunity; an Office of Financial Education; an Office of Service Member Affairs directed toward members of the military and their families; an Office of Financial Protection for Older Americans to, among other things, "facilitate the financial literacy of individuals who have attained the age of 62 years or more ... on protection from unfair, deceptive, and abusive practices on current and future financial choices";[61] and a Private Education Loan Ombudsman to, among other things, study and attempt to resolve complaints raised by private education loan borrowers.[62]

General Powers

The authorities of the Bureau fall into three broad categories: supervisory, which includes the power to examine and to impose reporting requirements on financial institutions; enforcement of various consumer protection laws and regulations; and rulemaking. Some of these powers are newly established by the Dodd-Frank Act, such as the authority to supervise nondepository financial institutions. A significant portion of the Bureau's powers were transferred from other regulators to the Bureau, including the authority to prescribe regulations under the enumerated consumer laws.

Covered Entities and Activities

Under the CFP Act, the Bureau has authority over an array of consumer financial products and services, including deposit taking, mortgages, credit cards and other extensions of credit, loan servicing, check guaranteeing, collection of consumer report data, debt collection associated with consumer financial products and services, real estate settlement, money transmitting, financial data processing, and others.[63] While the breadth of the products, services, and entities that fall

---

(...continued)

Recess Appointments Clause of the U.S. Constitution and the statutory authorities these individuals may exercise, which are discussed in CRS Report R42323, *President Obama's January 4, 2012, Recess Appointments Legal Issues*, by David H. Carpenter et al.

[60] 12 U.S.C. §1. The Comptroller of the Currency also serves for a five-year term and may be "removed by the President, upon reasons to be communicated by him to the Senate." 12 U.S.C. §2. Other financial regulators that are headed by single directors are the Federal Housing Finance Agency (regulator of Fannie Mae, Freddie Mac, and the Federal Home Loan Banks) (12 U.S.C. §4512) and, the former regulator, OTS (12 U.S.C. §1462a). Other financial regulators are set up as commissions or boards. These include the FDIC (12 U.S.C. §1812), the Securities and Exchange Commission (15 U.S.C. §78d), the FTC (15 U.S.C. §41), the FRB (12 U.S.C. §241), and the NCUA (12 U.S.C. §1725a). See, also, Senate Report No. 111-176, p. 161 (2010) (explaining that the CFPB's executive and administrative structures "are modeled on similar statutes governing the Office of the Comptroller of the Currency and the Office of Thrift Supervision, which are located within the Department of the Treasury.").

[61] Dodd-Frank Act §1013, 12 U.S.C. §5493.

[62] Dodd-Frank Act §1035, 12 U.S.C. §5535.

[63] Dodd-Frank Act §1002(15), 12 U.S.C. §5481(15). The Bureau also has authority over "service providers," which generally includes individuals that provide "a material service to a covered person in connection with the offering or (continued...)

---

within the Bureau's jurisdiction is considerable, the CFP Act imposes some important exceptions to and limitations on the CFPB's rulemaking, enforcement, and supervisory powers. In some instances, the CFP Act clearly defines the institutions that the Bureau may regulate.[64] In other cases, the statutory language establishes less objective standards that provide the CFPB a fair amount of discretion to determine the types of institutions that may fall within its regulatory jurisdiction.[65] How the Bureau interprets and applies these standards could significantly affect the scope of the Bureau's powers and the impact that the Bureau's actions have on consumer financial markets.

Depositories With More Than $10 Billion in Assets

As is described in greater detail above,[66] the banking regulators traditionally have regulated the depository institutions under their jurisdictions for both safety and soundness and consumer compliance. The CFP Act significantly departs from this traditional model with respect to depository institutions holding more than $10 billion in assets ("larger depositories"). The CFP Act transfers from the banking regulators to the Bureau the primary consumer compliance supervisory, enforcement, and rulemaking authority over larger depositories.[67] The safety and soundness supervisory, enforcement, and rulemaking authority over these institutions remains with their banking regulators (i.e., the OCC, FRB, FDIC, or NCUA).

The Bureau's supervisory powers include the authority to examine larger depositories for consumer compliance, meaning that the CFPB has visitorial[68] powers over larger depositories that historically have been almost exclusively held by their prudential banking regulators. The CFP Act, however, does require the Bureau to coordinate examinations and other supervisory activities with larger depositories' state and federal prudential regulators, and it establishes a procedure for resolving conflicts between the Bureau and a prudential regulator.[69] Furthermore, the Bureau may

---

(...continued)

provision of a consumer financial product or service...." Dodd-Frank Act §1002(26), 12 U.S.C. §5481(26).

[64] E.g., depository institutions holding more than $10 billion in assets. Dodd-Frank Act §1025, 12 U.S.C. §5515.

[65] E.g., nondepository financial institutions that are "larger participant[s] in a market." Dodd-Frank Act §1024, 12 U.S.C. §5514.

[66] See the "Federal Consumer Financial Protection Regulation Before the CFPB" section of this report.

[67] Dodd-Frank Act §§1061-1067, 12 U.S.C. §§5581-5587.

[68] 12 C.F.R. Section 7.4000 defines visitorial powers to include

    (i) Examination of a bank;

    (ii) Inspection of a bank's books and records;

    (iii) Regulation and supervision of activities authorized or permitted pursuant to federal banking law; and

    (iv) Enforcing compliance with any applicable Federal or state laws concerning those activities, including through investigations that seek to ascertain compliance through production of non-public information by the bank [subject to certain exceptions]....

See, also, Guthrie v. Harkness, 199 U.S. 148, 158 (1905) ("Visitation, in law, is the act of a superior or superintending officer, who visits a corporation to examine into its manner of conducting business, and enforce an observance of its laws and regulations. [Alexander M.] Burrill defines the word to mean 'inspection; superintendence; direction; regulation.'" (Burrill authored legal dictionaries often used at the time of the case.)).

[69] Dodd-Frank Act §1025, 12 U.S.C. §5515.

require reports directly from larger depositories, although it will have to rely on existing reports "to the fullest extent possible."[70]

As a supervisor, the Bureau has an important responsibility of safeguarding non-public information of financial institutions. Through the exercise of its examination and reporting powers, the CFPB (much like banking regulators) may acquire sensitive competitive, commercial, and personal information, as well as evidence of practices that may violate state or federal law. This information could be useful to private litigants, state attorneys general, and market competitors. However, the banking regulators have long protected much of this information from being shared with third parties so as to encourage bank officials to openly provide information without the fear of private lawsuits and to maintain a competitive marketplace.[71] This information also is exempt from public disclosure under the Freedom of Information Act.[72] As a result, parties without examination and other supervisory powers generally have only been able to gain access to proprietary and confidential bank information through litigation.[73] Rules of procedure and evidence associated with litigation serve as significant barriers to access of banks' non-public information, and stand in stark contrast to the supervisory powers of the banking regulators and now the CFPB.

In 2011, the Bureau issued rules that govern how it will handle confidential information acquired through its regulatory actions and the extent to which that information may be shared with individuals and state and federal regulators outside of the CFPB.[74] These rules are very similar, though not identical, to analogous rules prescribed by the banking regulators.[75] Despite their similarity with existing confidentiality rules of the banking regulators, some have expressed concern that the CFPB will be more willing to share non-public bank information, especially with state attorneys general to aid investigations and enforcement actions.[76] These concerns seem to be stoked by at least a couple of issues. One is that the CFPB may exercise its supervisory and enforcement powers over larger depositories with a primary statutory focus on consumer compliance, rather than concentrating on the impact that such actions may have on the institutions' safety and soundness.[77] The second is the Bureau has actively pursued partnerships

---

[70] Dodd-Frank Act §1025, 12 U.S.C. §5515.

[71] See, e.g., 12 C.F.R. §4.36 ("It is the OCC's policy regarding non-public OCC information that such information is confidential and privileged. Accordingly, the OCC will not normally disclose this information to third parties.").

[72] 5 U.S.C. §552(b)(8) (exempting from public disclosure, information "contained in or related to examination, operating, or condition reports prepared by, on behalf of, or for the use of an agency responsible for the regulation or supervision of financial institutions....").

[73] See, generally, CRS Report R40595, *Cuomo v. The Clearing House Association, L.L.C National Banks Are Subject to State Lawsuits to Enforce Non-Preempted State Laws*, by M. Maureen Murphy.

[74] Disclosure of Records and Information, 76 Fed. Reg. 45,372 (July 28, 2010) (codified at 12 C.F.R. pt. 1070).

[75] E.g., *compare id. with* the OCC's regulations on the release of non-public information, 12 C.F.R. §§4.31-4.40.

[76] See, e.g., Melanie Hibbs Brody, Paul F. Hancock, David G. McDonough, Jr., and Stephanie C. Robinson, *And the Plot Thickens the CFPB Issues A Quartet of Interim Final Rules Laying Out Its Investigatory and Enforcement Procedures*, Aug. 16, 2011, available at http://www.klgates.com/and-the-plot-thickens-08-16-2011/. A separate area of concern involves the affect that submitting documents to the Bureau as part of the regulatory process will have on the attorney-client and other privileges. For more information on this subject, see Confidential Treatment of Privileged Information, 76 Fed. Reg. 15,286 (Mar. 15, 2012) and the public comments to the proposal.

[77] See, generally, Thomas P. Vartanian, *All You Need to Know About CFPB Exam Is in the Manual*, American Banker, Feb. 13, 2012, available at http://www.americanbanker.com/bankthink/all-you-need-to-know-about-CFPB-exam-is-in-the-manual-1046629-1.html?zkPrintable=true. Sharing non-public information in some instances may create litigation risk or cause reputational harm that may negatively impact an institution's safety and soundness.

with state attorneys general as a means to enhance consumer protection.[78] For example, the CFPB and the Presidential Initiative Working Group of the National Association of Attorneys General announced a Joint Statement of Principles, in which they agreed to, among other things,

- Share information, data, and analysis about conduct and practices in the markets for consumer financial products or services to inform enforcement policies and priorities;

- Engage in regular consultation to identify mutual enforcement priorities that will ensure effective and consistent enforcement of the laws that protect consumers of financial products or services;

- Support each other, to the fullest extent permitted by law as warranted by the circumstances, in the enforcement of the laws that protect consumers of financial products or services, including by joint or coordinated investigations of wrongdoing and coordinated enforcement actions; [and]

- Pursue legal remedies to foster transparency, competition, and fairness in the markets for consumer financial products or services across state lines and without regard to corporate forms or charter choice for those providers who compete directly with one another in the same markets;....[79]

Only time will tell whether the Bureau will handle confidential information in much the same way as banking regulators have in the past or whether it will share information with state prosecutors or other third parties more freely.

Depositories With $10 Billion or Less in Assets

The Bureau's supervisory and enforcement authority over depositories with $10 billion or less in assets (smaller depository institutions) is far more limited than its powers over larger depositories. The CFP Act does not transfer the primary consumer protection supervisory or enforcement powers over smaller depository institutions to the CFPB; those authorities remain with the prudential banking regulators.

However, the Bureau does have some limited back-up supervisory authority over smaller depository institutions. For instance, the Bureau, "on a sampling basis," may participate in examinations of smaller depository institutions that are conducted by prudential regulators.[80] The prudential regulators must provide the CFPB access to all reports, records, and other documents connected to the examination; must allow the CFPB examiners to participate in all aspects of the examination; and generally must take into account any input that the CFPB's examiner offers

---

[78] Melanie Hibbs Brody, Paul F. Hancock, David G. McDonough, Jr., and Stephanie C. Robinson, *And the Plot Thickens the CFPB Issues A Quartet of Interim Final Rules Laying Out Its Investigatory and Enforcement Procedures,* Aug. 16, 2011, available at http://www.klgates.com/and-the-plot-thickens-08-16-2011/.

[79] Consumer Financial Protection Bureau and National Association of Attorneys General Presidential Initiative Working Group Release Joint Statement of Principles, CFPB Press Release, Apr. 11, 2011, available at http://www.consumerfinance.gov/pressrelease/consumer-financial-protection-bureau-and-national-association-of-attorneys-general-presidential-initiative-working-group-release-joint-statement-of-principles/.

[80] Dodd-Frank Act §1026(c), 12 U.S.C. §5516(c).

---

regarding the examination. Also, the Bureau may require reports directly from these depositories, although the Bureau will have to rely on existing reports "to the fullest extent possible."[81]

The CFP Act does not provide the Bureau enforcement powers over smaller depository institutions, although the new law does establish a formal procedure by which the Bureau can refer potential enforcement actions against smaller depository institutions to their prudential regulators. The relevant banking regulator would have to respond to the referral but would not be bound to take any other substantive steps associated with it.[82]

Smaller depositories generally will be subject to the consumer protection rules that are prescribed by the Bureau.

Nondepository Financial Institutions

The CFP Act does not provide the Bureau with jurisdiction over all nondepository financial institutions. Rather, the CFP Act authorizes the CFPB to regulate providers of three explicit categories of consumer financial products and services, as well as entities that meet one of two discretionary standards. The act explicitly provides the Bureau authority over providers of private student loans, providers of payday loans,[83] and entities that engage in mortgage-related activities, such as mortgage origination, brokerage, mortgage servicing, mortgage modification, and foreclosure relief activities.[84]

The two more flexible standards include any entity that the Bureau considers to be a "larger participant in a [consumer financial] market,"[85] as well as any entity that the Bureau has reasonable cause to believe is "engaging, or has engaged, in conduct that poses risks to consumers with regard to the offering or provision of consumer financial products or services." [86] Rather than rigidly constraining the Bureau's authority to an exhaustive list of institutions and activities, these flexible standards may provide the Bureau the latitude to evolve with the markets by, for example, making it possible to regulate entities that offer consumer financial products or services were not in the marketplace when the Dodd-Frank Act was signed into law. On the other hand, this discretion could create uncertainty for those nondepository financial institutions that do not clearly fall within one of these categories. Concerns associated with this uncertainty might be alleviated if, for example, the CFPB establishes a policy of providing a considerable amount of time between the date on which an institution is determined to be subject to the Bureau's supervision and the date on which such an entity will be directly impacted by the supervision.

---

[81] Dodd-Frank Act §1026(b), 12 U.S.C. §5516(b).

[82] Dodd-Frank Act §1026(d), 12 U.S.C. §5516(d).

[83] While the Bureau has authority to regulate payday lenders, it does not have authority to set usury limits. Dodd-Frank Act §1027(o), 12 U.S.C. §5517(o). Some consumer advocates have argued that interest rate caps are the only proven way to effectively curb predatory practices of payday lenders. Center for Responsible Lending, *Issue Brief Payday Loans Put Families in the Red*, Feb. 2009, available at http://www.responsiblelending.org/payday-lending/research-analysis/payday-puts-families-in-the-red-final.pdf ("Payday lending industry representatives have lobbied for other reforms, such as payment plans and renewal bans, because they understand that these measures have done nothing to slow the rate at which they can flip loans to the same borrowers. But an interest rate cap is the only measure that has proven effective.").

[84] Dodd-Frank Act §1024, 12 U.S.C. §5514.

[85] As determined by the Bureau in regulations after consultation with the FTC. Dodd-Frank Act §1024, 12 U.S.C. §5514.

[86] Dodd-Frank Act §1024, 12 U.S.C. §5514.

The Bureau has the authority to require any company that falls into one of these categories (a "covered nondepository") to register with the Bureau, to submit to examinations, to submit to background checks, and to adhere to other measures designed "to ensure that such persons are legitimate entities and are able to perform their obligations to consumers."[87] However, the Bureau generally must coordinate examinations with any other state and federal regulators that have supervisory authority over covered nondepositories and must rely on existing reports required by those regulators "to the fullest extent possible." The Bureau generally shall serve as the primary enforcer of federal consumer financial laws with respect to covered nondepositories and has primary consumer protection rulemaking authority over such entities.

As previously mentioned, covered nondepositories historically have not been subject to up-front supervision at the federal level. As result, the Bureau's examination, reporting, and other supervisory powers over covered nondepository financial institutions is a significant change from past federal regulation that largely took the form of *ex post* enforcement. These powers give the CFPB the potential to regulate covered nondepositories in an analogous fashion to banks, thrifts, and credit unions. In so doing, the Bureau potentially could eliminate the competitive forces between depositories, nondepositories, and their regulators that some believe led to the "regulatory arbitrage" and "race-to-the-bottom" problems discussed above.

Nondepository Institutions with Explicit Exemptions

The Dodd-Frank Act explicitly exempts a number of entities from the CFPB's jurisdictional reach, such as automobile dealers and accountants. However, the statutory language defining the scope of several of these exemptions is complex and includes subjective standards, such as "regularly extends" and "engaged significantly," that the Bureau might decide to expound on in future guidance and regulations.

Merchants, Retailers, and Sellers of Nonfinancial Goods and Services

For example, the Bureau generally does not have authority to regulate merchants, retailers, and sellers of non-financial goods and services, even if such an entity extends credit to borrowers for the purchase of their goods and services.[88] However, these entities could engage in certain business practices that would trigger CFPB regulatory authority.

The CFPB could regulate a merchant, retailer, and seller of nonfinancial goods or services if such an entity "regularly extends credit and the credit is subject to a finance charge" and is "engaged significantly in offering or providing consumer financial products or services."[89] Such an entity also could become subject to the CFPB's regulatory authority if it either (1) "assigns, sells or otherwise conveys to another person such [nondelinquent] debt owed by a consumer," or (2) extends credit that "significantly exceeds the market value of the nonfinancial good or service

---

[87] Dodd-Frank Act §1024, 12 U.S.C. §5514.

[88] Dodd-Frank Act §1027(a), 12 U.S.C. §5517(a) ("Except as provided in subparagraph (B), and subject to subparagraph (C), the Bureau may not exercise any rulemaking, supervisory, enforcement, or other authority under this title with respect to a merchant, retailer, or seller of nonfinancial goods or services, but only to the extent that such person—(i) extends credit directly to a consumer ... exclusively for the purpose of enabling that consumer to purchase such nonfinancial good or service directly from the merchant, retailer, or seller; (ii) ... collects debt arising from [such] credit ... or (iii) sells or conveys [such] debt ... that is delinquent or otherwise in default.").

[89] Dodd-Frank Act §1027(a)(2), 12 U.S.C. §5517(a)(2).

provided" or otherwise evades the CFP Act.[90] However, the Bureau's rulemaking, supervisory, and enforcement authorities are further constrained over certain small businesses, as established by the Small Business Act,[91] that otherwise would only fall under the Bureau's jurisdiction because they "regularly extend[] credit and the credit is subject to a finance charge."[92] For example, a large furniture store with a national presence that occasionally allows customers to pay off the purchase of a bedroom set over the course of 12 months without additional charge, likely would not fall within the Bureau's jurisdictional reach. If that same furniture store charges interest over the 12 months, it is possible that the store could be regulated by the CFPB. However, a small, independently owned furniture store that regularly charges interest on furniture purchases that are paid off over 12 months may fall outside the Bureau's regulatory authority due to the CFP Act's exception for certain small businesses.

The Bureau also has authority over merchants, retailers, and sellers of nonfinancial goods or services to the extent that they fall within the ambit of an enumerated consumer law.[93]

In short, the Bureau's authority to supervise, prescribe regulations, and enforce consumer protection laws on merchants, retailers, and sellers of nonfinancial goods is limited, but not insubstantial. The extent to which the Bureau may regulate these institutions is based on subjective standards such as "regularly extends credit," "engaged significantly," and "significantly exceeds." Unless the Bureau provides greater guidance on how this language will be interpreted, merchants, retailers, and sellers may have difficulty determining whether or not they will be regulated by the CFPB and the extent to which they would have to modify their business practices and procedures to avoid regulation.

Automobile Dealers

The Bureau generally does not have supervisory, rulemaking, or enforcement powers over automobile dealers engaged in leasing, selling, or servicing automobiles. However, the Bureau may regulate financial activities engaged in by automobile dealers that are outside of the normal automobile dealer business. For example, the Bureau could regulate an automobile dealer to the extent that it extends credit directly to consumers rather than "routinely assign[ing the credit] to an unaffiliated third party finance or leasing source."[94] The CFPB also would have jurisdiction over automobile dealers that sell or offer to sell consumer financial products or services unrelated "to the sale, financing, leasing, rental, repair, refurbishment, maintenance, or other servicing of motor vehicles, motor vehicle parts, or any related or ancillary product or services."[95] This could include dealers that offer car title loans, payday loans, or mortgage-related products or services.

Although the Bureau's regulatory powers over automobile dealers are significantly constrained, the CFP Act streamlines the rulemaking process that the FTC must follow to issue unfair or deceptive trade practice rules against automobile dealers. Normally, when the FTC promulgates

---

[90] Dodd-Frank Act §1027(a)(2), 12 U.S.C. §5517(a)(2).

[91] 15 U.S.C. §632.

[92] Dodd-Frank Act §1027(a)(2)(D), 12 U.S.C. §5517(a)(2)(D). To qualify as a small business for the purposes of this provision, a merchant, retailer, or seller must meet the size thresholds that are provided by 15 U.S.C. §632.

[93] Dodd-Frank Act §1027(a)(1), 12 U.S.C. §5517(a)(1).

[94] Dodd-Frank Act §1029, 12 U.S.C. §5519.

[95] Dodd-Frank Act §1029, 12 U.S.C. §5519.

unfair or deceptive rules pursuant to Section 5 of the Federal Trade Commission Act (FTC Act),[96] it must adhere to the rigorous procedures of the Magnuson-Moss Act,[97] which include public hearings and publishing staff reports.[98] The CFP Act allows the FTC to issue these rules in accordance with the standard informal rulemaking procedures of the Administrative Procedure Act.[99] Thus, while automobile dealers generally are outside of the Bureau's authority, the CFP Act may make it somewhat easier for the FTC to regulate them.

Other Excluded Entities

The CFP Act also generally excludes from the Bureau's rulemaking, supervisory, and enforcement authority real estate brokers,[100] real estate agents,[101] sellers of manufactured and mobile homes,[102] income tax preparers,[103] and accountants[104] to the extent that they are acting in their normal capacity (e.g., a real estate broker is exempt to the extent that she brings parties together to purchase a property). However, the CFP Act authorizes some authority for the Bureau to regulate these entities if they extend credit; otherwise sell or offer to sell a consumer financial product or service; or engage in an activity that makes them subject to an enumerated consumer law.

Attorneys generally are exempt from the Bureau's supervisory and enforcement authority (although the act does not explicitly exempt attorneys from the Bureau's rulemaking authority) when they are practicing law. However, this exemption would not apply to the extent that an attorney sells or offers to sell "a consumer financial product or service ... that is not offered or provided as part of, or incidental to, the practice of law, occurring exclusively within the scope of the attorney-client relationship; or that is otherwise offered or provided by the attorney in question with respect to any consumer who is not receiving legal advice or services from the attorney in connection with such financial product or service."[105] Thus, the CFPB likely would not have authority to regulate an attorney who regularly extends financing to her clients explicitly for payment of legal services the attorney provided those clients. Additionally, the Bureau likely would not have authority to regulate an attorney who advances credit based on an expected legal settlement award to a client to buy a car if the attorney were hired in relation to the traffic accident that prompted the need for a new car. However, the CFPB likely could regulate an

---

[96] 15 U.S.C. §45.

[97] 15 U.S.C. §57a.

[98] See, Federal Trade Commission Operating Manual ch. 7.3, available at http://www.ftc.gov/foia/ch07rulemaking.pdf. Other steps include "an investigation oriented towards rulemaking," a staff report that "provide[s] sufficient reason for the Commission to conclude that corrective actions is warranted and that rulemaking is the enforcement method of choice," an advance notice of proposed rulemaking (ANPR) published in the *Federal Register*, making the information collected as part of the investigation available for public review, and publishing a final staff report. See, also, p. 3, note 23, of CRS Report R41546, *A Brief Overview of Rulemaking and Judicial Review*, by Vanessa K. Burrows and Todd Garvey.

[99] 5 U.S.C. §553. See, also, pp. 1-2 of CRS Report R41546, *A Brief Overview of Rulemaking and Judicial Review*, by Vanessa K. Burrows and Todd Garvey.

[100] Dodd-Frank Act §1027(b), 12 U.S.C. §5517(b).

[101] Dodd-Frank Act §1027(b), 12 U.S.C. §5517(b).

[102] Dodd-Frank Act §1027(c), 12 U.S.C. §5517(c).

[103] Dodd-Frank Act §1027(d), 12 U.S.C. §5517(d).

[104] Dodd-Frank Act §1027(d), 12 U.S.C. §5517(d).

[105] Dodd-Frank Act §1027(e), 12 U.S.C. §5517(e).

attorney who regularly converts structured legal settlements to lump sum payments for non-clients.

Other entities and activities that generally fall outside of the Bureau's jurisdictional reach include insurance companies;[106] employee benefit plans;[107] entities that are regulated by state securities commissions;[108] firms regulated by the Securities and Exchange Commission (SEC)[109] or the Commodity Futures Trading Commission (CFTC);[110] those regulated by the Farm Credit Administration;[111] and donations to tax-exempt charities.[112] The CFP Act also explicitly prohibits the Bureau from imposing interest rate caps (a.k.a., usury limits) on any loan or other extension of credit.[113]

Newly Established Rulemaking

The Dodd-Frank Act establishes procedures that the Bureau must follow when proposing and prescribing rules, in addition to the notice of proposed rulemaking and comment period procedures required for informal rulemakings under the Administrative Procedure Act and other generally applicable federal administrative laws.[114] The act also imposes additional procedures for specific types of rulemaking (e.g., when declaring certain acts or practices to be unfair or abusive), which are discussed below.

General Rulemaking Powers

The CFP Act authorizes the Bureau to "prescribe rules and issue orders and guidance, as may be necessary or appropriate to enable the Bureau to administer and carry out the purposes and objectives of the Federal consumer financial laws, and to prevent evasions thereof."[115] Before proposing a rule and during the comment period of a proposed rule, the CFPB is required to consult with the "appropriate" financial regulators.[116] The Bureau must address any written objections by the federal prudential regulators when issuing final regulations. Additionally, the CFPB must consider "the potential benefits and costs to consumers and covered persons, including the potential reduction of access by consumers to consumer financial products and services resulting from such rule," as well as the impact the rule would have on smaller depositories and "consumers in rural areas."[117]

---

[106] Dodd-Frank Act §1027(f), 12 U.S.C. §5517(f).

[107] Dodd-Frank Act §1027(g), 12 U.S.C. §5517(g).

[108] Dodd-Frank Act §1027(h), 12 U.S.C. §5517(h).

[109] Dodd-Frank Act §1027(i), 12 U.S.C. §5517(i).

[110] Dodd-Frank Act §1027(j), 12 U.S.C. §5517(j).

[111] Dodd-Frank Act §1027(k), 12 U.S.C. §5517(k).

[112] Dodd-Frank Act §1027(*l*), 12 U.S.C. §5517(*l*).

[113] Dodd-Frank Act §1027(o), 12 U.S.C. §5517(o).

[114] 5 U.S.C. §553. For a more detailed discussion of the Bureau's rulemaking procedural requirements, see CRS Report R41380, *The Dodd-Frank Wall Street Reform and Consumer Protection Act Regulations to be Issued by the Consumer Financial Protection Bureau*, by Curtis W. Copeland.

[115] Dodd-Frank Act §1022(b), 12 U.S.C. §5512(b).

[116] Dodd-Frank Act §1022(b), 12 U.S.C. §5512(b).

[117] Dodd-Frank Act §1022(b), 12 U.S.C. §5512(b).

Additionally, the CFP Act requires the Bureau to take a number of steps to evaluate the impact that proposed regulations may have on small businesses. More specifically, if the Bureau expects that a proposed rule will have a "significant economic impact on a substantial number of small entities,"[118] then it must offer a written analysis that describes, among other things,

> (A) any projected increase in the cost of credit for small entities; (B) any significant alternatives to the proposed rule which accomplish the stated objectives of applicable statutes and which minimize any increase in the cost of credit for small entities; and (C) advice and recommendations of representatives of small entities relating to issues described in subparagraphs (A) and (B)....[119]

Within five years of any CFPB "significant rule or order" becoming effective and after a public comment period, the Bureau must publish a report assessing the effectiveness of the rule or order.[120] The act does not specify what is to be considered "significant," presumably leaving these determinations to the Bureau.

The CFP Act also transfers to the CFPB rulemaking authority under the enumerated consumer laws.[121] In some instances, the Bureau will share rulemaking powers under the enumerated consumer laws with other financial regulators. For example, the CFPB has primary rulemaking authority under the Electronic Funds Transfer Act, but the FRB has exclusive authority to prescribe regulations to implement the debit interchange fee restrictions of Section 920 of that act, which is commonly referred to as the "Durbin Amendment."[122]

As a check on the Bureau's rulemaking powers, the Financial Stability Oversight Council (FSOC)—which is established under Title III of the Dodd-Frank Act and mainly composed of the federal financial regulators, including the Director of the Bureau[123]—has the ability to set aside or stay a regulation prescribed by the Bureau if the regulation "would put the safety and soundness of the United States banking system or the stability of the financial system of the United States at risk."[124] No other federal financial regulator is subject to a similar executive agency "veto" power, so there are no real analogs to look to for guidance on how frequently this power could be used. Because the FSOC is comprised of the heads of financial regulators with whom the CFPB generally must consult when crafting regulations, the Bureau likely will be aware of concerns of FSOC members about a proposed rule and likely will have the opportunity to allay those concerns before a rule is finalized, which may reduce the probability of the FSOC voting to overturn a rule.

---

[118] "Small entities" include small businesses, small organizations, and small governmental jurisdictions, as those terms are defined at 5 U.S.C. §601.

[119] 5 U.S.C. §603(d), as amended by Dodd-Frank Act §1100G. These requirements would not have to be met if the CFPB issued final regulations without issuing a notice of proposed rulemaking as allowed under certain circumstances pursuant to the Administrative Procedure Act. The Bureau, at times, also must convene an "advocacy review panel" pursuant to the Regulatory Flexibility Act. For a more detailed description of the Bureau's obligations under the Regulatory Flexibility Act, see p. 17 of CRS Report R41380, *The Dodd-Frank Wall Street Reform and Consumer Protection Act Regulations to be Issued by the Consumer Financial Protection Bureau*, by Curtis W. Copeland.

[120] Dodd-Frank Act §1022(d), 12 U.S.C. §5512(d).

[121] Dodd-Frank Act Title X, Subtitle H, 12 U.S.C. §§5581, *et seq.*

[122] 15 U.S.C. §1693b, as amended by Dodd-Frank Act §1084(3).

[123] The Director also will serve as an ex-officio member of the FDIC board. 12 U.S.C. §1812(f)(2), as amended by Dodd-Frank Act §336.

[124] Dodd-Frank Act §1023(a), 12 U.S.C. §5513(a).

Specific Rulemaking Powers

Unfair, Deceptive, or Abusive Acts or Practices

The CFP Act provides the Bureau the authority to prescribe rules declaring acts or practices pertaining to covered consumer financial products or services to be unlawful because they are unfair, deceptive, or abusive. This is a broad mandate that leaves the Bureau with a great deal of discretion to determine how to wield this power, in part, because of the inherent difficulty of objectively defining the terms "unfair," "deceptive," and "abusive." However, the Bureau's unfair, deceptive, and abusive rulemaking authority is very similar to the FTC's mandate under the FTC Act.[125] For example, the statutory language defining "unfairness" under the CFP Act is virtually identical to the FTC Act's standard of unfairness.[126] Thus, while it is not statutorily required to do so, the Bureau might look to the FTC's longstanding interpretation of the FTC Act when prescribing regulations under this new authority, to the extent that doing so also comports with the CFP Act.[127]

Although these two mandates are similar in many ways, there are some important distinctions between them. One is their scope. The Bureau's unfair, deceptive, and abusive authority is limited to consumer financial products and services and to those entities that fall under the Bureau's general regulatory jurisdiction. The FTC's authority applies to a broader universe of "acts or practices in or affecting commerce," as that phrase is defined in 15 U.S.C. Section 45.

A second important distinction is the procedural requirements that must be met before rules can be prescribed. When prescribing rules under Section 1023 of the Dodd-Frank Act, the Bureau must consult with the other federal financial regulators, as appropriate, and otherwise follow the general rulemaking procedures, as described above. The FTC, on the other hand, generally must follow the much more onerous, time consuming, and costly procedures of 15 U.S.C. Section 57a, commonly referred to as "Magnuson-Moss rulemaking" after the law that established them.[128]

---

[125] 15 U.S.C. §§41, *et seq.*

[126] *Compare* Dodd-Frank Act §1031, 12 U.S.C. §5531(the Bureau may not declare an act or practice unfair unless it has "a reasonable basis to conclude that the act or practice causes or is likely to cause substantial injury to consumers, which is not reasonably avoidable by consumers; and such substantial injury is not outweighed by countervailing benefits to consumers or competition.") *with* 15 U.S.C. §45(n) ("The [Federal Trade] Commission shall have no authority under this section or section 57a of this title to declare unlawful an act or practice on the grounds that such act or practice is unfair unless the act or practice causes or is likely to cause substantial injury to consumers which is not reasonably avoidable by consumers themselves and not outweighed by countervailing benefits to consumers or to competition.").

[127] See, e.g., FTC Policy Statement on Unfairness, Dec. 17, 1980, available at http://www.ftc.gov/bcp/policystmt/ad-unfair.htm and FTC Policy Statement on Deception, Oct. 14, 1983, available at http://www.ftc.gov/bcp/policystmt/ad-decept.htm.

[128] Magnuson-Moss Warranty—Federal Trade Commission Improvement Act, P.L. 93-637, 15 U.S.C. §57a. See, Federal Trade Commission Operating Manual ch. 7.3, available at http://www.ftc.gov/foia/ch07rulemaking.pdf. Required steps include "an investigation oriented towards rulemaking"; a staff report that "provide[s] sufficient reason for the Commission to conclude that corrective actions is warranted and that rulemaking is the enforcement method of choice"; an advance notice of proposed rulemaking (ANPR) published in the *Federal Register*, making the information collected as part of the investigation available for public review; and publishing a final staff report. See, also, p. 3, note 23, of CRS Report R41546, *A Brief Overview of Rulemaking and Judicial Review*, by Vanessa K. Burrows and Todd Garvey. As is discussed above, the FTC does not have to comply with the Magnusson-Moss rulemaking procedures to issue unfair or deceptive trade practice regulations against automobile dealers. Dodd-Frank Act §1029, 12 U.S.C. §5519. Although previous iterations of what would ultimately become the CFP Act modified the FTC's rulemaking procedures for declaring unfair or deceptive trade practices under Section 5 of the FTC Act, those changes were not (continued...)

Another distinction is the statutory use of the term "abusive." The FTC Act does not explicitly bar "abusive" acts or practices. As a result, the FTC has not provided longstanding guidance and commentary on the term's meaning from which the Bureau could draw.[129] The CFP Act does provide the Bureau statutory guidance on the term's meaning, although this statutory language is somewhat malleable. Under the CFP Act, an abusive act or practice may only be deemed unlawful by regulation if it

> materially interferes with the ability of a consumer to understand a term or condition of a consumer financial product or service; or takes unreasonable advantage of (a) a lack of understanding on the part of the consumer ...; (b) the inability of the consumer to protect the interests of the consumer in selecting or using a consumer financial product or service; or (c) the reasonable reliance by the consumer on a covered person to act in the interests of the consumer.[130]

The terms "materially interferes," "unreasonable advantage," and "reasonable reliance" could provide the Bureau the ability to regulate emerging business practices. At the same time, however, financial service providers may have to deal with the inherent uncertainty associated with the Bureau's future interpretation of the term "abusive."

Disclosure Requirements

The Bureau also has the authority to prescribe rules imposing disclosure requirements to help consumers understand the terms, benefits, costs, and risks of financial products and services. When prescribing these rules, the CFPB must follow the general rulemaking procedures described above and also must "consider the available evidence about consumer awareness, understanding of, and responses to disclosures or communications about the risks, costs, and benefits of consumer financial products or services."[131]

Rulemakings Initiated by the States

If a majority of states adopt a resolution requesting a new consumer protection regulation under the CFPB's jurisdiction or a change in an existing rule, the Bureau must issue a notice of proposed rulemaking on the subject. Before finalizing such a rule, the Bureau must assess whether or not the final rule will (1) increase consumer protection; (2) create more benefits than costs for consumers; (3) unfairly discriminate against a group of consumers; and (4) "likely [] present an unacceptable safety and soundness risk to insured depository institutions," if such a

---

(...continued)

included in the Dodd-Frank Act, as enacted.

[129] Other federal consumer protection laws under which the FTC historically has held rulemaking and enforcement authority do prohibit "abusive" practices. For example, Section 806 of the Fair Debt Collection Practices Act (15 U.S.C. §§1692, *et seq.*) prohibits debt collectors from engaging in conduct, "the natural consequence of which is to harass, oppress, or *abuse* any person in connection with the collection of a debt." 15 U.S.C. §1692d (emphasis added). The Telemarketing and Consumer Fraud and Abuse Prevention Act (15 U.S.C. §§6101 *et seq.*) also provides the FTC the authority to "prescribe rules prohibiting deceptive telemarketing acts or practices and other *abusive* telemarketing acts or practices." 15 U.S.C. 6102(a) (emphasis added). As a result, the FTC does have experience interpreting the terms "abuse" and "abusive" in contexts outside of the FTC Act. See, e.g., FTC Staff Commentary on the Fair Debt Collection Practices Act, 53 Fed. Reg. 50,097 (Dec. 13, 1988); 16 C.F.R. §310.4.

[130] Dodd-Frank Act §1031, 12 U.S.C. §5531.

[131] Dodd-Frank Act §1032, 12 U.S.C. §5532.

---

concern is raised by a prudential regulator. If the Bureau decides not to finalize such a rule, it must publish an explanation of the decision in the Federal Register.[132]

Rulemaking Under the Enumerated Consumer Laws

As previously mentioned, the CFPB acquired authority to prescribe regulations pursuant to a large group of federal consumer protection laws that largely predated the Dodd-Frank Act. Individually, these laws target discrete activities. Taken as a whole, these enumerated consumer laws govern a broad and diverse set of consumer activities and services including debt collection practices, debit card transfers, overdraft services, consumer leases, mortgage lending, credit card lending, mortgage appraisals, real estate settlement practices, and credit reporting, among others. As a result, the transfer of rulemaking authority under these laws represents a major source of the Bureau's regulatory powers. Although these consumer laws are predominately disclosure-oriented, they also include various substantive restrictions.[133]

The enumerated consumer laws are the Alternative Mortgage Transaction Parity Act;[134] the Consumer Leasing Act of 1976;[135] the Electronic Funds Transfer Act,[136] except with respect to Section 920;[137] the Equal Credit Opportunity Act;[138] the Fair Credit Billing Act;[139] the Fair Credit Reporting Act,[140] except with respect to Section 615(e) and Section 628;[141] the Homeowners Protection Act of 1998;[142] the Fair Debt Collection Practices Act;[143] subsections (b) through (f) of Section 43 of the Federal Deposit Insurance Act;[144] Section 502 through Section 509 of the Gramm-Leach-Bliley Act,[145] except for Section 505 as it applies to Section 501(b);[146] the Home Mortgage Disclosure Act of 1975;[147] the Home Ownership and Equity Protection Act of 1994;[148]

---

[132] Dodd-Frank Act §1041(c), 12 U.S.C. §5551(c).

[133] See, e.g., Truth in Lending Act, 73 Fed. Reg. 44,522 (July 30, 2008) (the FRB issued final regulations imposing a number of substantive restrictions on mortgage lending pursuant to the rulemaking authority of TILA §129*l*(2) (15 U.S.C. §1639(*l*)(2)).

[134] 12 U.S.C. §§3801, *et seq.*

[135] 15 U.S.C. §§1667, *et seq.*

[136] 15 U.S.C. §§1693, *et seq.*

[137] Section 920 of the Electronic Funds Transfer Act delineates the interaction between the EFTA and state laws. 15 U.S.C. §1693q.

[138] 15 U.S.C. §§1691, *et seq.*

[139] 15 U.S.C. §§1666, *et seq.*

[140] 15 U.S.C. §§1681, *et seq.*

[141] 15 U.S.C. §§1681m(e) and 1681w. These provisions primarily pertain to "red flag" identity theft prevention measures for federal financial institutions and credit report record retention by federal financial institutions.

[142] 12 U.S.C. §§4901, *et seq.*

[143] 15 U.S.C. §§1692, *et seq.*

[144] 12 U.S.C. §§1831t(c)-(f). These provisions pertain to disclosure requirements for depository institutions that do not hold federal deposit insurance.

[145] 15 U.S.C. §§6802-6809. These provisions deal with financial institutions' use and protection of non-public consumer information.

[146] This provision pertains to federal banking agency rulemaking applicable to the safeguarding of non-public personal information by banking concerns.

[147] 12 U.S.C. §§2801, *et seq.*

[148] 15 U.S.C. §1639.

the Real Estate Settlement Procedures Act of 1974;[149] the S.A.F.E. Mortgage Licensing Act of 2008;[150] the Truth in Lending Act (TILA);[151] the Truth in Savings Act;[152] Section 626 of the Omnibus Appropriations Act, 2009;[153] the Interstate Land Sales Full Disclosure Act;[154] and most provisions of the Mortgage Reform and Anti-Predatory Lending Act,[155] which was enacted as Title XIV of the Dodd-Frank Act.

The CFPB has not acquired rulemaking authority over all existing federal consumer protection laws. For example, the FTC retains its primary rulemaking authority under the FTC Act;[156] the banking regulators continue to hold rulemaking authority pursuant to the Community Reinvestment Act;[157] and HUD maintains its rulemaking authority under the Fair Housing Act.[158]

Funding

The Bureau's primary source of funding is not appropriations, like that of most executive agencies, or assessments on institutions within its regulatory jurisdiction, as is typical of federal banking regulators. Instead, the Bureau primarily is funded by a transfer of non-appropriated funds from the FRS's operating expenses, in an amount "determined by the Director to be reasonably necessary to carry out the authorities of the Bureau," subject to specified caps.[159] The cap will be 10% of the total operating expenses of the FRS for FY2011, 11% for FY2012, and 12% thereafter. The caps are based on the operating expenses as reported in the FRS's annual report for 2009 and are to be adjusted for inflation.[160] As a gauge of how much money this will be, the FRS's operating expenses for FY2009 totaled $4.98 billion, 10% of which is just under $500 million.[161] The statutory caps on the funds that may be transferred to the CFPB give the Bureau less flexibility than the OCC, FDIC, and other banking regulators that are able to increase assessments on the institutions within their jurisdiction to raise revenue, as needed to carry out their responsibilities.[162]

Because it does not rely on appropriations for funding, the Bureau is insulated, to some degree, from the uncertainties inherent to the congressional appropriations process. Congress does have

---

[149] 12 U.S.C. §§2601, *et seq.*

[150] 12 U.S.C. §§5101, *et seq.*

[151] 15 U.S.C. §§1601, *et seq.*

[152] 12 U.S.C. §§4301, *et seq.*

[153] P.L. 111-8, §626. This provision pertains to a regulation under which states may bring actions to enforce certain Truth in Lending Act requirements regarding mortgage loans.

[154] 15 U.S.C. §§1701, *et seq.*

[155] Dodd-Frank Act Title XIV, Subtitles A, B, C, and E, and §§1471, 1472, 1475, and 1476. See Dodd-Frank Act §1400.

[156] 15 U.S.C. §§41, *et seq.*

[157] 12 U.S.C. §§2901, *et seq.*

[158] 42 U.S.C. §§3601, *et seq.*

[159] Dodd-Frank Act §1017, 12 U.S.C. §5497.

[160] Dodd-Frank Act §1017, 12 U.S.C. §5497.

[161] Federal Reserve System's 96th Annual Report, 2009, available at http://www.federalreserve.gov/boarddocs/ rptcongress/annual09/pdf/AR09.pdf.

[162] See, e.g., 12 U.S.C. §§482, 1817(b).

---

many other ways of exerting influence over and conducting oversight of the Bureau's budget outside of the typical appropriations process. The CFP Act, for example, requires the Bureau to submit semi-annual reports to Congress that provide, among other things, a justification of its budget requests. A minimum of twice each year, the Bureau Director must appear before the Senate Committee on Banking, Housing, and Urban Affairs, the House Committee on Financial Services, and the House Committee on Energy and Commerce.[163] The Bureau also must submit certain financial information for Office of Management and Budget review and is subject to regular audits by the Comptroller General.[164] Of course, Congress could pass legislation that subjects the Bureau's budget to additional congressional scrutiny, including the appropriations process.[165]

In addition to the transfer of funds from the FRS, the act authorizes appropriations if the Director "determine[s] that sums available to the Bureau [as specified by the caps] under this section will not be sufficient to carry out the authorities of the Bureau under Federal consumer financial law for the upcoming year." Upon the Bureau's making such a finding and submitting a report to both the House and Senate Committees on Appropriations, the CFP Act provides authorization for an appropriation of $200 million per year for FY2010-FY2014.[166] To date, the CFPB has not requested appropriated funds nor have any funds been appropriated to the Bureau.

The act also establishes a Consumer Financial Civil Penalty Fund for civil penalties secured by the Bureau for violations of consumer financial protection laws. The fund is to be used to pay victims of such violations, as well as for financial literacy and consumer education programs.[167]

Conclusion

The CFP Act significantly enhances federal consumer protection regulatory authority over nondepository financial institutions, potentially subjecting them to analogous supervisory, examination, and enforcement standards that have been applicable to depository institutions in the past. The act also transfers to the Bureau much of the consumer compliance authority over larger depositories that previously had been held by banking regulators. Additionally, the Bureau acquired the authority to write rules to implement most federal consumer financial protection laws that previously was held by a number of other federal agencies. Although the powers that the CFPB has at its disposal are largely the same or analogous to those that other federal regulators have held for decades, there is uncertainty in how the Bureau will exercise these broad and flexible authorities, especially in light of its almost exclusive focus on consumer protection.

---

[163] Dodd-Frank Act §1016, 12 U.S.C. §5496.

[164] Dodd-Frank Act §1017(a), 12 U.S.C. §5497(a); P.L. 112-10 §1573(c), 12 U.S.C. §5496a.

[165] H.R. 2434, the Financial Services and General Government Appropriations Act, 2012, for example, would require the CFPB to be funded through appropriations after FY2012.

[166] Dodd-Frank Act §1017(e), 12 U.S.C. §5497(e).

[167] Dodd-Frank Act §1017(b), 12 U.S.C. §5497(b).

Author Contact Information

David H. Carpenter
Legislative Attorney
dcarpenter@crs.loc.gov, 7-9118